BODY AND MIND
LGBTQ HEALTH ISSUES

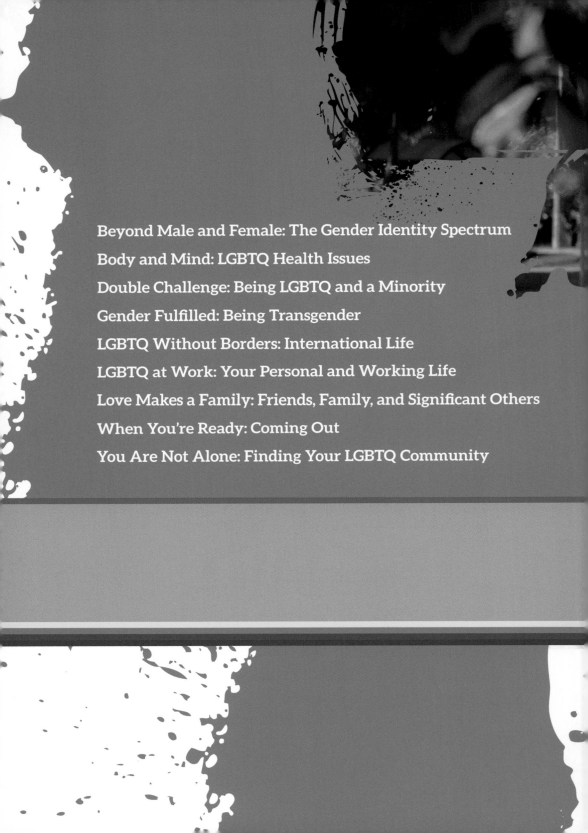

LGBTQ
LIFE

BODY AND MIND
LGBTQ HEALTH ISSUES

By Jeremy Quist

Mason Crest
Philadelphia • Miami

Mason Crest
450 Parkway Drive, Suite D
Broomall, PA 19008
(866) MCP-BOOK (toll free)
www.masoncrest.com

Printed in the United States of America
First printing
9 8 7 6 5 4 3 2 1
Series ISBN: 978-1-4222-4273-5
Hardcover ISBN: 978-1-4222-4275-9
E-book ISBN: 978-1-4222-7522-1

Cataloging-in-Publication Data is available on file at the Library of Congress.

Developed and Produced by Print Matters Productions, Inc. (www.printmattersinc.com)

Cover and Interior Design by Tim Palin Creative

QR CODES AND LINKS TO THIRD-PARTY CONTENT

CONTENTS

KEY ICONS TO LOOK FOR

WORDS TO UNDERSTAND: These words, with their easy-to-understand definitions, will increase readers' understanding of the text while building vocabulary skills.

SIDEBARS: This boxed material within the main text allows readers to build knowledge, gain insights, explore possibilities, and broaden their perspectives by weaving together additional information to provide realistic and holistic perspectives.

EDUCATIONAL VIDEOS: Readers can view videos by scanning our QR codes, providing them with additional educational content to supplement the text.

TEXT-DEPENDENT QUESTIONS: These questions send the reader back to the text for more careful attention to the evidence presented there.

RESEARCH PROJECTS: Readers are pointed toward areas of further inquiry connected to each chapter. Suggestions are provided for projects that encourage deeper research and analysis.

SERIES GLOSSARY OF KEY TERMS: This back-of-the-book glossary contains terminology used throughout this series. Words found here increase the reader's ability to read and comprehend higher-level books and articles in this field.

I'm so excited that you've decided to pick up this book! I can't tell you how much something like this would have meant to me when I was in high school in the early 2000s. Thinking back on that time, I can honestly say I don't recall ever reading anything positive about the LGBTQ community. And while *Will & Grace* was one of the most popular shows on television at the time, it never made me feel as though such stories could be a reality for me. That's in part why it took me nearly a decade more to finally come out in 2012 when I was 25 years old; I guess I knew so little about what it meant to be LGBTQ that I was never really able to come to terms with the fact that I was queer myself.

But times have changed so much since then. In the United States alone, marriage equality is now the law of the land; conversion therapy has been banned in more than 15 states (and counting!); all 50 states have been served by an openly LGBTQ-elected politician in some capacity at some time; and more LGBTQ artists and stories are being celebrated in music, film, and on television than ever before. And that's just the beginning! It's simply undeniable: *it gets better.*

After coming out and becoming the proud queer person I am today, I've made it my life's goal to help share information that lets others know that they're never alone. That's why I now work for the It Gets Better Project (www.itgetsbetter.org), a nonprofit with a mission to uplift, empower, and connect LGBTQ youth around the globe. The organization was founded in September 2010 when the first It Gets Better video was uploaded to YouTube. The viral online storytelling movement that quickly followed has generated over 60,000 video stories to date, one of the largest collections of LGBTQ stories the world has ever seen.

Since then, the It Gets Better Project has expanded into a global organization, working to tell stories and build communities everywhere. It does this through three core programs:

- **Media.** We continue to expand our story collection to reflect the vast diversity of the global LGBTQ community and to make it ever more accessible to LGBTQ youth everywhere. (See, itgetsbetter.org/stories.)
- **Global.** Through a growing network of affiliates, the It Gets Better Project is helping to equip communities with the knowledge, skills, and resources they need to tell their own stories. (See, itgetsbetter.org/global.)
- **Education.** It Gets Better stories have the power to inform our communities and inspire LGBTQ allies, which is why we're working to share them in as many classrooms and community spaces we can. (See, itgetsbetter.org/education.)

You can help the It Gets Better Project make a difference in the lives of LGBTQ young people everywhere. To get started, go to www.itgetsbetter.org and click "Get Involved." You can also help by sharing this book and the other incredible volumes from the LGBTQ Life series with someone you know and care about. You can also share them with a teacher or community leader, who will in turn share them with countless others. That's how movements get started.

In short, I'm so proud to play a role in helping to bring such an important collection like this to someone like you. I hope you enjoy each and every book, and please don't forget: *it gets better.*

Justin Tindall
Director, Education and
Global Programming
It Gets Better Project

Introduction

There is nothing fundamentally different about LGBTQ people, their bodies, or their brains. We're all human. We all have to worry about our health. Everyone has to make sure that they eat healthy and exercise. All people have to look after their sexual and mental health, as well. But LGBTQ people do face unique challenges that can make their efforts to preserve their health more difficult.

A large number of these problems are rooted in the discrimination, bullying, rejection, and violence that many LGBTQ people experience. These negative influences have a dramatic effect on a person's mental health, which impacts many other aspects of a person and their health, including their general well-being and their sexual health.

Most schools require some type of studies in the area of health. Many also require a program of sex education of some sort, although those programs can vary widely among different schools. This book does not intend to repeat the important things you will be learning in those classes. Instead, it seeks to fill in some of the holes that traditional health education leaves, because most of those classes exclude information that applies specifically to issues affecting LGBTQ people.

This isn't about special treatment. The difference in issues facing LGBTQ youth are quantifiable, meaning you can put numbers to them. Scientific research shows that LGBTQ people are at a heightened risk of mental illness due to the way they are still treated in our society, which will be discussed in Chapter 2. As a result of mental health challenges, they have higher rates of drug use, alcohol abuse, smoking, and other self-destructive behaviors, which will be discussed in Chapter 1. Chapter 3 goes into the unique sexual health issues LGBTQ people face, including higher rates of STIs (sexually transmitted infections); it also provides information that is generally left out of traditional sex ed classes. In Chapter 4, you will learn more about HIV/AIDS, including how the disease affects the body and the history of the AIDS crisis. LGBTQ people also face issues other people don't in accessing health care that is sensitive to their unique needs, so Chapter 5 seeks to help young LGBTQ people find appropriate mental and sexual health care services in their area.

WHAT IS MENTAL HEALTH?

The importance of mental health will be a recurring theme in this book. But the term *mental health* can confuse the issue sometimes. Some mental health issues stem from a natural defect in a person's brain. But that doesn't mean that there's something inherently wrong with the person.

Most of the time, including in the context of this book, when a person talks about mental health, they're talking about emotional health. You may not think of your brain as being subject to damage from things that occur around you, but we all can definitely acknowledge that our emotions can be greatly affected by others. That emotional strain can then in turn affect our bodies. Emotions affect health. That's what we mean when we talk about mental health.

There are some problems that people might have due to how their brain naturally functions, but those are not the types of problems that LGBTQ people are more prone to than the average person, so that's not what will be discussed in this book.

WHAT IS SEXUAL HEALTH?

Sexual health essentially means having a healthy relationship with one's own sexuality. That means knowing what risks a person faces to their health as a consequence of sex and knowing how to act upon that information. Information about sex is presented in this book, not just for its own sake or to make anyone uncomfortable, but to help people make the decisions that will help them preserve their health.

A NOTE ABOUT TERMS USED IN THIS BOOK

Some common terms used in this book may be unfamiliar to some people. *LGBTQ* refers to lesbian, gay, bisexual, transgender, and queer (or questioning). *Lesbian* refers to women who are attracted to women. *Gay* is usually used to refer to men who are attracted to other men, but it can be used to refer to lesbians as well, or occasionally the community as a whole. *Bisexuality* is when a person is attracted to both men and women. *Transgender* refers to a person who identifies as the opposite gender of what they were assigned at birth. And *queer* can be interpreted to mean other sexual and gender minorities, like asexual, pansexual, genderqueer, agender, and many others. Other terms will be defined as we go.

The unique health issues facing LGBTQ youth are quantifiable.

1

HEALTHY LIVING

WORDS TO UNDERSTAND

ANABOLIC STEROID: An artificial form of testosterone that some athletes use illegally for the purpose of gaining muscle.

CDC: The U.S. Centers for Disease Control and Prevention, a government agency that conducts research about many types of diseases and their prevention.

SELF—DESTRUCTIVE BEHAVIOR: Any action people take that is harmful to themselves—anything from eating poorly to actively harming oneself.

SELF—IMAGE: The way persons perceive themselves, whether it's accurate or not.

Of course, there are plenty of health issues that LGBTQ people share with others. Healthy living is healthy living, and a lot of what you will learn in health class in school applies to LGBTQ people in exactly the same way as to everyone else. Everyone needs to be aware of their diet and levels of physical activity. Diet and exercise affect most aspects of a person's health, even their mental health. Of course, staying active and eating healthy are sometimes more easily said than done.

The key to staying physically active is finding an activity you genuinely enjoy. For some, that's a team sport like football, soccer, baseball, or many others. Others find solitary activity more enjoyable, like running or hiking. Of course, it's also possible to mix the social element with non-team sports, like running with a friend or joining a gym buddy to encourage each other's weight lifting. Gym-based fitness is a popular route for gay men to take. LGBTQ sports teams are also becoming increasingly common, which can be a great way to connect with other people, find community, and get exercise at the same time.

Eating well is similar in that it sometimes takes some experimentation to find something that works for you. If you hate kale, you don't have to eat it to be healthy. There are plenty of other healthy food options out there. Just find the ones you can actually enjoy.

One healthy living habit that many people overlook is healthy sleeping patterns. According to the UCLA Sleep Disorders Center, the average adolescent needs approximately nine hours of sleep a night. Unfortunately, the average amount of sleep that teenagers get is about seven hours. There are a lot of pressures on the time of teenagers. Among school, homework, extracurricular activities, maintaining a social life, exercise (hopefully), maybe a part-time job, and many other obligations, it can be difficult to find enough time to sleep. But studies show that finding the time to sleep can help a person be healthier, happier, and more alert.

For LGBTQ people, who face external factors that can cause extra stress, stress management techniques can be especially useful. We've already covered a few things that help: healthy eating, exercise, and getting plenty of sleep. A lot of stress management involves pretty simple techniques like taking deep breaths when facing something that is causing stress. For some people, yoga, meditation, and other centering techniques can help relieve stress.

LGBTQ organized leagues exist for a wide variety of sports.

VARSITY GAY LEAGUE

LGBTQ-oriented leagues exist for a wide variety of sports, so if you want to keep going with track or football or softball after you finish high school, you definitely can! But what if you haven't really specialized in one sport while growing up, but you want to stay active and meet people while doing so?

Well, there's a league for that, too. The Varsity Gay League includes a wide variety of competitive pursuits. According to the organization's Web site, it offers "kickball, tennis, bowling, dodgeball, soccer, beach volleyball, trampoline dodgeball, trivia, beer olympics, game nights, paintball, capture the flag, and more."

The league is inclusive of all orientations and gender identities, has thousands of members, and has teams in cities around the country. You can check it out at www.varsitygayleague.com.

HOW TO DO IT WRONG

All people have ways in which they go against what they know is good for them. It can be something as simple as eating ice cream when you know you're lactose intolerant, or eating too much pizza when you know it's going to hurt your stomach. We all have some ways in which we're a little bit self-destructive. But not all **self-destructive behavior** is made equal. Some kinds are much worse than others.

LGBTQ people face certain difficulties in life that create added stress, including discrimination, bullying, and even violence to a greater degree than others. These hazards can create a number of mental health issues, which will be discussed more in Chapter 2, but for now we'll just point out that these added pressures can often lead LGBTQ people to a number of self-destructive behaviors in regard to their health.

LGBTQ people experience higher rates of smoking, alcohol abuse, drug abuse, steroid use, and eating disorders. All of these are self-destructive behaviors that are symptoms of the added stress and pressure of being an LGBTQ person in a society that still does not fully accept them. Of course, just because there are reasons for these behaviors to be common does not mean that they have to be there. Hopefully, the upcoming generation will be the one to break the pattern of unhealthy habits and actions.

To break the pattern, it's important to know the problems and the effects they have on people.

SMOKING AND VAPING

LGBTQ people are more likely to be smokers than the general population. The Truth Initiative says that 20 percent of LGB people and 35 percent of transgender people are smokers. That's compared to 15 percent for the general population. LGBTQ people are also more likely to be exposed to secondhand smoke, since they hang out with other LGBTQ people who are more likely to be smokers. They're also more likely to hang out at bars, where social tobacco use is more common, where it's still legal. In addition, "LGB individuals are 5 times more likely than others to never intend to call a smoking cessation quitline," according to the Centers for Disease Control (**CDC**).

All people have ways in which they go against what they know is good for them.

You're probably already aware of the health issues related to smoking, including cancer, lung disease, heart disease, and addiction.

Part of the reason for the high rate of tobacco use in the community is due to the additional stress upon LGBTQ people facing societal pressures. Some of it also has to do with tobacco company marketing that specifically targets LGBTQ people. In response, some government agencies and anti-smoking organizations have begun campaigns aimed at discouraging LGBTQ people from smoking.

LGBTQ people were also early adopters of vaping and e-cigarettes. The nicotine contained in them is addictive and also poses special risks for brain development in young people. According to the CDC, "Using nicotine in adolescence can harm the parts of the brain that control

People tend to over use alcohol because it's considered to be what a person does for fun.

attention, learning, mood, and impulse control." The brain continues developing until a person is around 25 years old, so nicotine use during any of that time can impair your brain development.

ALCOHOL ABUSE

In the early years of the LGBTQ rights movement, bars were some of the few places that sexual and gender minorities might have had some expectation of being left alone, while finding others like them. Gay bars have existed for over a hundred years in some larger cities in the United States. They were never completely safe spaces, but they were the closest things available. As a result, bars and clubs have become fixtures within the queer subculture. It's not surprising, then, that LGBTQ people drink at a higher rate than the average person.

Alcohol can have its place in a healthy person's life. It's legal for adults over 21, and many, many healthy people enjoy an alcoholic beverage now and again. But it's also tragically common for people to over-indulge. Even separate from the issue of addiction, which will be covered in the next chapter, some people over-use alcohol just because it's considered to be what a person does for fun.

Research suggests that marijuana can impair the development of the brain in young people.

Whether you're an alcoholic or not, consuming a ton of alcohol has extreme effects on your body. The most impacted parts are your liver, heart, and brain, but the damage doesn't end there. Even mental illness can be triggered or made more intense by alcohol use. Alcohol is especially destructive to the developing brains of young people. As mentioned, your brain continues to develop until you're around 25, so any time before that, the things you do and consume can affect your brain for the rest of your life.

Ecstasy is not safe or harmless, in spite of what some people might tell you.

MARIJUANA

Cannabis is becoming legal in an increasing number states in the United States. Much of this is due to research that has shown that for adults, the health impacts are significantly lower than from other substances, like alcohol and tobacco, that are already legal. That applies to adults, but there is some research that suggests that marijuana, like alcohol and other substances, can impair the development of the brain in young people, affecting brain function, temperament, and mental health.

OTHER DRUG USE

Drug use is a major problem in the LGBTQ community. "LGBTQ youth are ... twice as likely to use ecstasy and cocaine, and four times as likely to use heroin and meth," according to LGBTQ Health Link (www.lgbthealthlink.org).

Ecstasy is often considered by people to be a mostly "safe" party drug, but health research shows a number of problems associated with it. Also called *MDMA*, ecstasy can refer to many different drug combinations. It's rarely possible to know exactly what chemicals you take into your body when you take ecstasy. The drug has been shown to be associated with memory loss, brain impairment, and mood problems. It's not safe or harmless, unlike some people might tell you.

Cocaine is nothing to mess around with either. According to the National Institute on Drug Abuse, "Severe medical complications can occur with cocaine use. Some of the most frequent are cardiovascular effects, including disturbances in heart rhythm and heart attacks; neurological effects, including headaches, seizures, strokes, and coma; and gastrointestinal complications, including abdominal pain and nausea." Of course, overdose is always a danger as well.

Severe medical complications can occur with cocaine use.

Heroin and meth have been incredibly devastating to millions of people who have used them. Not only are they incredibly destructive to the body, but they are so addictive that many people have completely lost everything to them. The addiction leads to people losing everything they have in pursuit of another high. There is nothing casual or recreational about using heroin or meth.

Within the LGBTQ community, there is often a bias placed upon appearance, which can be harmful.

It may seem that a little bit of drug use is a mostly harmless way to party with friends, but these are substances that have impacted the lives of LGBTQ people in countless ways. They are threats to the lives and health of the community.

All of these drugs have a negative impact on a person's mental health. People often begin taking drugs to escape their problems, but drug use only makes them worse.

Are Sexuality and Substance Abuse Correlated Within the LGBTQ Community?

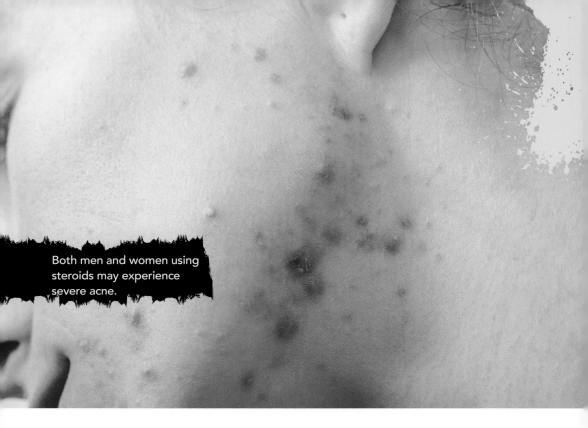

Both men and women using steroids may experience severe acne.

SELF-IMAGE AND STEROIDS

In the LGBTQ subculture, there is often an emphasis placed upon appearance, which can be harmful. While a focus on health and fitness can be a good thing, sometimes the pressures to look athletic and fit can lead to problems with a person's **self-image**, which in turn can lead people to some self-destructive behaviors. For some people, that means developing an eating disorder and/or body dysmorphia, both of which will be discussed in Chapter 2. For others, it can lead to obsessive exercising. Some go so far as to take steroids in the pursuit of increasing their muscle mass. LGBTQ people, including teenagers, are more likely than others to use steroids, which constitutes a major health danger. The many potential side effects include acne and infertility.

Side Effects of Steroids

The steroids typically used by athletes are an artificially created form of testosterone. According to the Mayo Clinic, **anabolic steroids** have serious physical side effects:

Men may develop

- Prominent breasts
- Shrunken testicles
- Infertility
- Prostate gland enlargement

Women may develop

- A deeper voice, which may be irreversible
- An enlarged clitoris, which may be irreversible
- Increased body hair
- Baldness, which may be irreversible
- Infrequent or absent periods

Both men and women might experience

- Severe acne
- Increased risk of tendonitis and tendon rupture
- Liver abnormalities and tumors
- High blood pressure (hypertension)
- Heart and blood circulation problems
- Aggressive behaviors, such as rage or violence
- Psychiatric disorders, such as depression
- Drug dependence
- Infections or diseases such as HIV or hepatitis (for those who inject the drugs)
- Inhibited growth and development, and risk of future health problems in teenagers

The increased risk of self-destructive behaviors among LGBTQ people has to stop.

BREAKING THE PATTERN

There's no reason that the increased risk of self-destructive behaviors among LGBTQ people has to continue. It just takes individuals deciding not to let the societal pressures facing them drive them to hurt themselves.

For more information, or if you suffer from addiction, reach out to a doctor or counselor. The sooner you break the pattern, the better.

Yoga, meditation, and other centering techniques can help relieve stress.

TEXT-DEPENDENT QUESTIONS

1. Name a few self-destructive behaviors that impact LGBTQ people at a higher-than-average rate.

2. Around what age does the brain finish developing?

3. What are anabolic steroids? What effects do they have on the body?

RESEARCH PROJECTS

1. In what areas could you improve your health? Set some specific goals to help you improve in those areas.

2. Research one of the drugs discussed above: ecstasy, cocaine, heroin, or meth. List the effects that drug has on the human body and any risk of addiction that may be associated with using it.

2

Healthy Mind

WORDS TO UNDERSTAND

BODY DYSMORPHIA: *An obsession with one's personal appearance not based in reality, which is extreme enough that affects the person's everyday life.*

INTERNALIZED HOMOPHOBIA: *When a gay person is homophobic, whether consciously or subconsciously. Internalized biphobia, transphobia, and other variations are possible as well.*

STIGMA: *A negative perception attached to a person or a thing.*

David grew up in a very small, rural town. His family was very religious, and so were most of the people around him. The dominant view among his family, their religion, and the town as a whole was that being LGBTQ is not okay. "From a very young age, I was told that gay people were some of the worst of the worst people out there," he says. "It sunk deep into my brain— how I viewed the world and how I viewed myself. Even before I really realized that I was gay, these messages destroyed my self-image. I hated myself. I believed them when they said I was horrible."

Many people feel uncomfortable talking about mental health issues.

David began his struggles with depression in junior high school, but it wasn't until he was in his mid-20s, around the time he came out of the closet, that he sought mental health care. "I had gotten to the point where I was in genuine danger of hurting myself. If I hadn't finally reached out for help, I'm really scared to think about where I could have ended up."

He has since been diagnosed with a mood disorder and anxiety and takes medication for both. "I used to feel embarrassed talking about mental health issues, but I don't anymore," David says. "I wish I had started talking about them earlier because as soon as I did, my life started getting better."

When asked whether the attitude toward LGBTQ people he was exposed to as he grew up was a factor in his mental health problems, David says, "Oh, definitely. That was absolutely a major factor. Would I have had depression or mood issues anyway? Who knows? Maybe. But there's no question that the things I was told about gay people when I was a kid made things infinitely worse."

Negative attitudes toward LGBTQ people affect their mental health.

STIGMA AND MENTAL HEALTH

David is not unique. LGBTQ people face problems that other people are much less likely to face. Many are rooted in the fact that society still doesn't fully accept them. LGBTQ people experience discrimination, persecution, and violence in many aspects of life. The **stigma** attached to LGBTQ people by society directly affects mental health.

Research has shown that LGBTQ people in areas that are less accepting have higher rates of depression, mood disorders, and suicide than those in areas that are more accepting. It's not that there is something inherently wrong with these people; it's just the body's way of coping with stress and negative external factors.

It seems obvious to say that negative attitudes toward LGBTQ people will affect their mental health, but some people still don't see it that way. Some still argue that the higher rates of mental illness among sexual and gender minorities are proof of an underlying moral flaw instead of the logical result of being demoralized and discriminated against.

LGBTQ people are also more likely to face instability in their lives, which has major impacts upon mental health. For example, 42 percent of homeless youth are LGBTQ. Many more young LGBTQ people face the potential of losing their families if they come out of the closet. Many others face constant fear of bullying and discrimination. It would be ridiculous to expect them to have mental health issues at the same rate as straight youth.

The messages that we receive during our growing-up years become a major part of how we relate to the world around us.

INTERNALIZED HOMOPHOBIA

For everyone, the messages that we receive during our growing-up years become a major part of how we relate to the world around us. They're tough messages to get rid of. Often, they become so entrenched in our heads that they lead to what is most often called **internalized homophobia**, but the principle also applies to internalized biphobia and transphobia. The basic idea is that internalized homophobia is when a gay person is homophobic, sometimes even after they have come out of the closet and think that they've come to terms with their sexuality. All of the terrible things that they've heard growing up have stuck in their heads, and part of them still believes it.

Internalized homophobia can come in the form of negative messaging about oneself, like calling oneself homophobic names in one's head. It also can come in the form of generalizing about other gay people to criticize the gay community as a whole (and talk negatively about oneself by association), or to criticize individual groups within the community. It's okay to look at the community with a critical eye to help improve it, but when it takes on the hateful tone that others would use, it's a symptom of internalized homophobia.

Depression can be an excruciating experience that takes over a person's life.

DEPRESSION AND SUICIDE

Sadly, one of the most prevalent problems among LGBTQ youth is depression and the sometimes associated issue of suicide. Here are the most heartbreaking statistics you'll read in this book: according to the Human Rights Campaign (HRC), "28 percent of LGBTQ youth—including 40 percent of transgender youth—said they felt depressed most or all of the time during the previous 30 days, compared to only 12 percent of non-LGBTQ youth . . . LGBQ young people are more than twice as likely to feel suicidal, and over four times as likely to attempt suicide, compared to heterosexual youth . . . the rates may be especially high for bisexual teens. According to one study, a third of transgender youth have seriously considered suicide, and one in five has made a suicide attempt."

Everyone feels sad sometimes, but depression as a mental health issue is when that sadness doesn't go away and begins to impact a person's everyday life. According to the American Psychiatric Association:

Depression symptoms can vary from mild to severe and can include the following:
Feeling sad or having a depressed mood
Loss of interest or pleasure in activities once enjoyed
Changes in appetite—weight loss or gain unrelated to dieting
Trouble sleeping or sleeping too much
Loss of energy or increased fatigue
Increase in purposeless physical activity (e.g., hand-wringing or pacing) or slowed movements and speech (actions observable by others)
Feeling worthless or guilty
Difficulty thinking, concentrating, or making decisions
Thoughts of death or suicide

Depression can be an excruciating experience that takes over a person's life. It should be taken very seriously, both in yourself and in others, especially if you think there may be a chance it could lead to suicide.

The Trevor Project specializes in LGBTQ youth mental health support.

The best way to deal with depression is to reach out for help. If you feel you can, ask your parents or school counselor for help. If those options are not available, you should try to find mental health services in your area or online. For options in finding LGBTQ-friendly health services, refer to Chapter 5.

Another great option is the Trevor Project (www.thetrevorproject. org), which specializes in LGBTQ youth mental health support. They have a hotline you can call at 866-488-7386. There is also a text option you can try by sending "START" to 678678. The Web site gives you the option to instant message a counselor.

Another great resource for some is an accepting community within their school. That could mean simply a person's circle of friends who are aware of their problems and support them. Many schools also have a GSA (Genders and Sexualities Alliance) of LGBTQ people and their allies, where a person may be able to find someone who can relate to their feelings.

If you're worried about depression in another person, reach out to them. Let them know that you support them and care about them. Help them find professional help.

THE STIGMA TOWARD MENTAL HEALTH

A strong person has the strength of character to ask for help when they need it.

If you were repeatedly punched until your nose were broken, and your eyes were swollen shut, no one would think you were weak for going to see a doctor. But if you are mentally and emotionally beaten down, time and time again every day, some people perceive seeking help for that type of wound as a sign of weakness. It's just not true.

LGBTQ people can be especially sensitive to this bias against mental health care. As the National Alliance on Mental Illness (NAMI) says, "LGBTQ people must confront stigma and prejudice based on their sexual orientation or gender identity while also dealing with the societal bias against mental health conditions. Some people report

How Discrimination Leads to Mental Health Challenges

having to hide their sexual orientation from those in the mental health system for fear of being ridiculed or rejected. Some hide their mental health conditions from their LGBTQ friends." The combination of stigmas can work together to prevent LGBTQ people from getting the care they need.

Everyone needs help at some point in their lives—physical help, emotional help, or any other kind. Pretending that's not true does not make a person strong. A strong person has the strength of character to ask for help when they need it.

EATING DISORDERS

The cultural attitudes toward appearance that are common in the LGBTQ community, mixed with the social and mental health pressures they already face, create a severe problem with body image and healthy eating habits. Eating disorders can take many forms, including anorexia (when a person doesn't eat enough), bulimia (when a person forces themself to vomit the food they've eaten), compulsively exercising while not eating enough calories to fuel their exercise, misuse of laxatives, and more.

Eating disorders are devastating to the body.

According to research conducted by the Trevor Project, over half of LGBTQ youth between the ages of 13 and 24 who were surveyed had been diagnosed with eating disorders at some point in their lives—54 percent—with an additional 21 percent believing that they probably have had an eating disorder at some point without being diagnosed.

Eating disorders are devastating to the human body. Most obviously, a person's digestive system is extremely impacted, preventing the body from incorporating nutrients, which can have long-term consequences. Other normal functions of the body are affected in extreme ways, including those of the brain, heart, and immune system. Sexual health is impacted as well, through a drop in the production of testosterone and estrogen, as well as irregular menstruation. Hair loss and extremely low energy levels can occur, as can many other effects, all the way up to death. The list of the health impacts of eating disorders is too long to include it here.

According to the National Eating Disorder Association (NEDA), the best way to deal with eating disorders is to reach out for counseling and help from health professionals. "People struggling with an eating disorder need to seek professional help. The earlier a person with an eating disorder seeks treatment, the greater the likelihood of physical and emotional recovery." Eating disorders are not to be taken lightly. If you are struggling with one, contact a doctor or mental

Causes of Eating Disorders

The National Eating Disorder Association (NEDA) says that many external factors that LGBTQ people face are common causes of eating disorders, including

- Fear of rejection or experience of rejection by friends, family, and co-workers
- Internalized negative messages or beliefs about oneself due to sexual orientation, non-normative gender expressions, or transgender identity
- Experiences of violence and post-traumatic stress disorder (PTSD), which research shows sharply increases vulnerability to an eating disorder
- Discrimination because of one's sexual orientation and/or gender identity
- Being a victim of bullying because of one's sexual orientation and/or gender identity
- Discordance between one's biological sex and gender identity
- Inability to meet body image ideals within some LGBTQ cultural contexts

Pursuing impossible body image
ideals can lead to anorexia.

Body dysmorphia occurs when a person becomes obsessed with what they perceive as physical flaws.

health professional in your area, or contact the Trevor Project at www. thetrevorproject.org.

BODY DYSMORPHIA

Related to eating disorders, but different in significant ways, is the problem of **body dysmorphia**. Sometimes called *body dysmorphic disorder*, or BDD, body dysmorphia occurs when a person becomes obsessed with what they perceive as physical flaws. The disorder is related to obsessive-compulsive disorders (OCDs) in that the obsession with their appearance often becomes so intense that their everyday life is affected.

In the sidebar, you can read about how body dysmorphia affected the life of the actor Reid Ewing. For Reid, body dysmorphia led to a problem with multiple plastic surgeries, but it can manifest itself in many different ways, such as an obsession with working out, picking at the skin, or even just spending a lot of time focused on a particular part of the body.

For LGBTQ people who feel pressure to look a certain way and live up to often unrealistic expectations, body dysmorphia can be easy to fall into. Like with eating disorders, the best way to overcome body dysmorphia is to seek help from mental health professionals.

Body dysmorphia isn't logical.

SUBSTANCE ABUSE AND ADDICTION

LGBTQ adults are nearly twice as likely as the general population to have substance abuse issues—15 percent to 8 percent, according to research by the HRC. Like the other issues LGBTQ people face as a group, a complex combination of factors lead to this higher rate. For one, substance abuse is often tied to depression and other mental health issues. But addiction (as compared to casual drug use) is also something a person can be genetically prone to. Addiction ruins lives, both of the addicts themselves and their loved ones. People

Actor Reid Ewing's Struggle to Overcome Body Dysmorphia

Actor Reid Ewing is best known for his role in *Modern Family*, where he plays Haley's cute but sometimes airheaded on-again-off-again boyfriend. But in his everyday life, the openly gay actor says that he believed he was too hideous to be content with himself. In an article he wrote for the *Huffington Post*, Reid says he thought, "No one is allowed to be this ugly."

He thought this while being cast in a role defined partly by his good looks! But body dysmorphia isn't logical and doesn't respond to other people's opinions of a person's appearance.

As a result of his body dysmorphia, Reid underwent a series of cosmetic surgeries, beginning at the age of 19. But the surgeries never made him look the way he thought he ought to look. He continued to find flaws and reasons to go back for more surgery.

After years of this cycle, Reid came to the understanding that this "was clearly a psychological issue." He broke his addiction to trying to change himself even though he was still not thoroughly comfortable with how he looked. With time, he came to regret having any surgeries at all and learned to accept his appearance as it was.

LGBTQ adults are nearly twice as likely as the general population to have substance abuse issues.

lose control over themselves and are unable to stop their self-destructive behavior.

The best way to avoid addiction is to avoid entirely all of the things that we all know very well are addictive substances. You may think it's just for fun, but it can quickly spiral out of control. Why risk it?

If addiction already affects you, seek out mental health care services as soon as you can.

The It Gets Better Project speaks powerfully to the ability of LGBTQ people to make their lives better.

It Gets Better

Depression is often made worse by the thought that things are never going to improve. We think that our current state of unhappiness will just be our reality forever. To combat that hurtful (and false) idea, writer and advocate Dan Savage began the movement known as It Gets Better. He started with his husband in a video in which they share very personal experiences about how their lives improved after growing up and coming out.

In the years since then, hundreds of other people, including celebrities and regular people, have shared their own stories of overcoming hopelessness and depression. Taken together, the movement speaks powerfully of the ability of LGBTQ people to make their lives better.

To see stories of people like you, go to www.itgetsbetter.org or www.youtube.com/user/itgetsbetterproject.

TEXT-DEPENDENT QUESTIONS

1. What is internalized homophobia?

2. What is body dysmorphia?

3. What are some external factors that can cause an eating disorder?

RESEARCH PROJECTS

1. Imagine you find out that a friend is severely depressed. What would you do to help them? Beginning with the resources provided here, research ways to help someone who is struggling with depression. Write out what your strategy for helping your friend would be.

2. Imagine you find out that a friend has a substance abuse problem. What would you do to help them? Beginning with the resources provided here, research ways to help someone who is struggling with addiction. Write out what your strategy for helping your friend would be.

3

Sexual Health for LGBTQ People

WORDS TO UNDERSTAND

HETERONORMATIVE: *Anything that forwards the idea that heterosexual is the "normal" or preferred way for people to be.*

KINSEY SCALE: *A way to express the range of human sexual behavior, first developed by Alfred Kinsey.*

MSM: *Men who have Sex with Men—a term used in health care to refer to sexual behavior instead of how a person identifies, for the purpose of determining health risk.*

STIs: *Sexually transmitted infections (sometimes referred to as STDs).*

Sexual education is a controversial issue in the United States. Some people feel that more information about sex should be provided to young people; others feel that talking about it can be harmful. Some

Sexual education is a controversial issue in the United States.

It's becoming clearer that a broader range of sexual education is needed.

people believe that sex education should be focused on teaching abstinence, while others think that strategies for preventing **STIs** (sexually transmitted infections) should be emphasized. Either way, sex education in school is almost always **heteronormative**, meaning that it assumes that heterosexuality is the "normal" way of doing things. It focuses entirely on issues relating to heterosexual people and heterosexual sex. Sex education for LGBTQ people is overlooked.

According to the CDC, 8 percent of high-school students identify as lesbian, gay, or bisexual. That doesn't include those who participate in same-sex activity without defining themselves that way. Numbers on trans and gender nonconforming young people are harder to come by, but estimates range from less than 1 percent to 3 percent. It's becoming clearer and clearer that a broader range of sexual education is needed.

Interestingly, a large majority of American parents also support the idea of having more inclusive sex ed in the schools. A study conducted by the HRC found that "85 percent of parents supported discussion of sexual orientation as part of sex education in high school." Compare that to the 12 percent of LGBTQ youth who say that they've "received information about safe sex that was relevant to them as an LGBTQ person." It's just a very vocal minority that keeps issues related to sexual and gender minorities out of sexual education.

Of course, a knowledge of how reproduction occurs is important for everyone to have, as is a general knowledge of common STIs. But a focus on contraception (preventing pregnancy) can seem less relevant to some LGBTQ people. For example, only talking about condom use as contraception can make it seem like something that only people having heterosexual sex have to worry about. But condoms can also make homosexual activity safer by making STI infection less likely.

SEXUAL BEHAVIOR VERSUS SEXUAL AND GENDER IDENTITY

It's important to understand the difference between a person's sexual behavior and their sexual identity. Sexual identities in this context are labels such as "gay," "bisexual," or "lesbian." Although there is certainly often a tie between these labels and sexual behavior, they are not the same thing. Sometimes someone's sexual behavior does not align perfectly with their identity, and that's normal.

People can think of themselves as heterosexual (and could very well be so!), while also having sexual encounters with someone of the same gender. For example, a man can have sexual encounters with another man and be aware that gay men are at increased risk of things like HIV. But he doesn't consider himself gay, so he thinks it doesn't affect him. It may seem obvious, but the way people see themselves is a powerful thing.

As one way to clarify the issue, sexual health professionals refer to **MSM**, which stands for *men who have sex with men*, instead of talking

People can think of themselves as heterosexual but still have sexual encounters with people of the same gender.

Young lesbians are at a heightened risk of unwanted pregnancy.

about gay or bisexual men. It puts the focus on a person's sexual behavior, which is what determines their risk of STIs, not their identity.

Young lesbians, meanwhile, are at a heightened risk of unwanted pregnancy. This is because their sexual identity leads them to not worry about contraceptives and birth control. Then when their sexual behavior doesn't 100 percent match their sexual identity, they're less prepared for preventing pregnancy.

Similarly, it is not a person's gender identity that determines risk of sexual health issues, but it is the sexual behavior that person engages in. Transgender women and men who have sex with men are at an increased risk of many STIs, and transgender men at the beginning stages of their transition should keep in mind that they can still become pregnant when having sex with a man.

SEXUALITY AS A SPECTRUM

A person's sexual attraction and behavior are not multiple-choice questions with only three responses: gay, straight, and bisexual. It's a much more complicated issue than that. Most people are not 100 percent gay or straight but lie somewhere on a spectrum, often referred to as the **Kinsey Scale** after Alfred Kinsey, the first sex researcher to bring the idea to public awareness. Kinsey proposed a scale of 0 to 6, with 0 being entirely heterosexual and 6 being entirely homosexual. His research found that surprisingly few people fell at a 0 or 6, with most people somewhere in between.

It's very normal for people to experiment with different sexual identities and behaviors.

A scale with only seven options is still a simplification of the broad range of human experience, of course, but it makes clear the limited usefulness of rigid labels and definitions of real people. Sex research consistently shows that it's very normal for people to experiment with different sexual identities and behaviors, particularly when they're first figuring out where their identities lie.

Gender identity can also lie on a spectrum, with some people not identifying 100 percent with either male or female. People are transgender when they think that their body is on the opposite end of the spectrum from their identity, but sometimes people can't really relate to either end of the spectrum. There are a number of labels that people might choose to express that, like *agender* or *genderqueer*.

Remember: when thinking about your sexual health risks, consider your sexual activity, not how you define yourself.

Condoms can be used for any kind of penetrative sex.

Safer Sex for LGBTQ People

Anyone who has sexual contact with anyone else is at some risk of being exposed to an STI, but there are some ways to reduce the chances of getting something. You already know that condoms can be used during heterosexual sex, because that's what is taught in sex ed. As mentioned, that includes those who participate in heterosexual sex without identifying that way. But their applications go beyond that. Condoms can be used for any kind of penetrative sex, meaning any sex act in which a body part or object penetrates a person's vagina, anus, or mouth.

For anyone who participates in anal sex, condoms are an important way to reduce risk. Don't think this part only applies to gay men. Plenty of people have anal sex who do not identify that way. That can include trans women, bisexual men, bisexual women, trans men, and anyone else who experiments with it despite their identity ... not to mention heterosexual men and women. Though less common,

Using a condom the wrong way decreases its usefulness in preventing STIs.

condoms can also be used for oral sex on a man or a trans woman who has a penis.

Condoms are often used incorrectly. Using a condom the wrong way decreases its usefulness in preventing STIs. Make sure to read the instructions on the package very carefully. If you have a penis and intend to have sex, you should practice putting the condom on without a partner. That way, you won't be nervous and fumbling and doing it the wrong way when the time comes.

Another important preventive measure when having anal sex is lubrication. Anal sex can cause small tears in the interior lining of the receptive partner (the "bottom" in gay slang). Those tears make transmission of STIs more likely. Lube makes it less likely that tearing will occur, making infection less likely as well.

For lesbians, bisexual women, and transgender men, the sharing of sex toys can lead to the transmission of STIs. One way to prevent this is by using condoms on the toys. Another is to clean them with diluted bleach: one part bleach to ten parts water. Though less common, dental dams can be used as a safer sex practice when performing oral sex on a woman or a trans man with a vagina. The sharing of sex toys among gay and bisexual men, transgender women, and heterosexual men and women happens less often, but it's something to keep in mind for them as well.

KNOW YOUR RISK, GET TESTED, AND GET TREATED

The various types of STIs are usually covered extensively by school sex education, so they won't be discussed at length here. But the point should not be to scare anyone or make them feel guilty. The point is to know what the risk is to your sexual health. From there, you can get tested for any STIs you may have been exposed to.

The LGBTQ Sex Talk

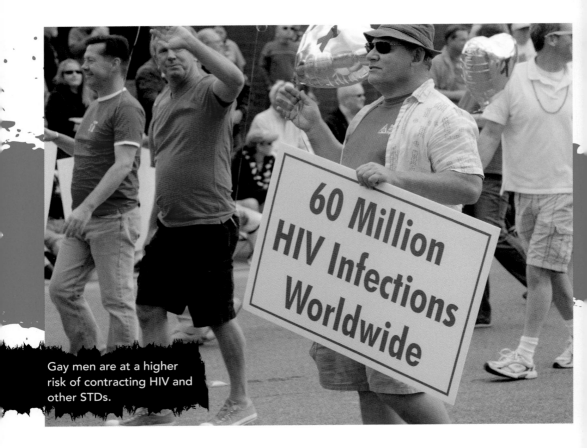

Gay men are at a higher risk of contracting HIV and other STDs.

Then, if something is diagnosed, you can seek treatment. And then life goes on.

Sexuality, gender, ethnicity, and economic factors combine in complex ways to complicate a person's risk factors. Of course, every person is their own individual, but researchers have identified some patterns that are useful in helping them prevent STIs in those groups. Some groups of people have a higher statistical probability of certain STIs and should be aware of that to protect themselves accordingly.

According to the U.S. Office of Disease Prevention and Health Promotion, "Gay men are at higher risk of HIV and other STDs, especially among communities of color." This disparity is due to "social discrimination and cultural issues," says the CDC. "Social and economic factors, including homophobia, stigma and lack of access

The CDC provides guidelines for what individuals should be tested for.

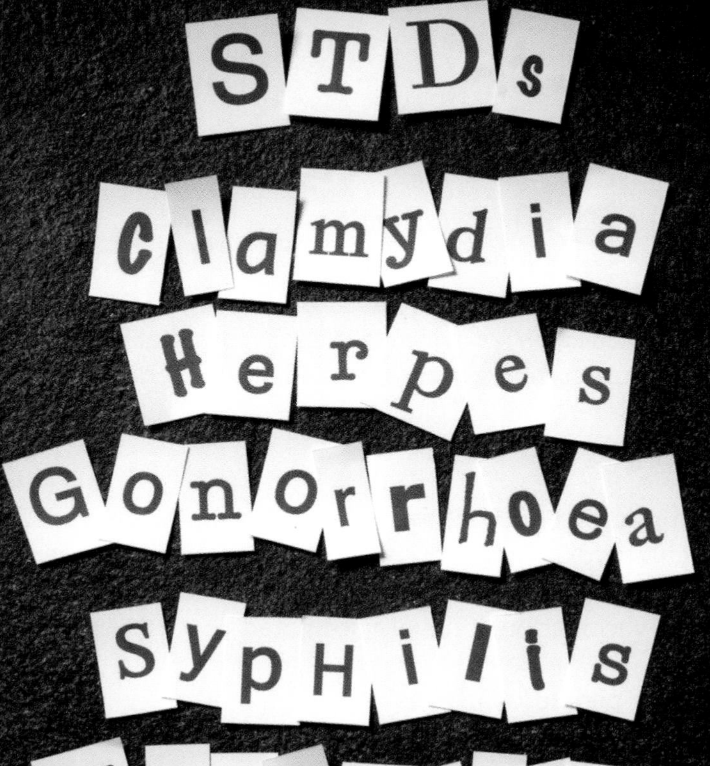

STDs

Clamydia

Herpes

Gonorrhoea

Syphilis

Hepatitis

Condyloma

HIV AIDs

to health care may increase risk behaviors or be a barrier to receiving HIV prevention services." The largest number of new HIV diagnoses in the U.S. are among African American MSM, followed by Latinos and whites, according to the CDC. (HIV/AIDS will be discussed in greater depth in the next chapter.)

WHAT SHOULD I GET TESTED FOR?

The U.S. government's Centers for Disease Control and Prevention (https://gettested.cdc.gov/) provides guidelines for what individuals should be tested for, based upon their gender, age, and sexual behavior. The age of 16 is used just as a point of reference.

16-year-old women:

- HIV testing at least once for everyone between the ages of 13 and 64
- Annual chlamydia and gonorrhea tests for women younger than 25 or with risk factors such as new or multiple sex partners
- Hepatitis B vaccination, if never vaccinated

Transgender people (of all ages):

- HIV testing (at least once annually)
- Screening for other sexually transmitted infections should include syphilis, gonorrhea, chlamydia, genital herpes, and hepatitis B and hepatitis C, as recommended by your health care provider.

16-year-old MSM (men who have sex with men):

- HIV at least once a year. Some may benefit from more frequent testing (e.g., every three to six months).
- Syphilis, chlamydia, and gonorrhea (at least once annually)
- The CDC suggests extragenital testing for all sexually active gay and bisexual men. Talk to your provider.
- Hepatitis A and hepatitis B vaccination

Strategies for accessing sexual health care are discussed in Chapter 5.

The risk of contracting STIs is not a reason to fear sexual activity.

Sex education for LGBTQ people is too often overlooked.

STI AND FEAR OF SEX

The mere existence of STIs is not a reason to fear sexual activity. Sex is a normal part of human experience. However, it's important to be aware of the ways that experience could negatively impact your life, and it's important to try to decrease your chances of experiencing those negative impacts.

Be aware of what your risk factors are, based upon your sexual activity. Check out the CDC's guidelines for you in the inset. From there, you can seek appropriate sexual health services based upon your risk and get tested. Guidance on finding health services will be given in Chapter 5.

TEXT-DEPENDENT QUESTIONS

1. What is the difference between sexual behavior and sexual identity?

2. Why is the difference between sexual behavior and sexual identity important?

3. What does *heteronormative* mean?

4. In what situations would a condom be useful?

RESEARCH PROJECTS

1. Use the CDC's Get Tested Web site (www.gettested.cdc.gov) to determine which tests you should receive on your next trip to the doctor.

2. Put some thought into where you lie on the Kinsey Scale. What are the implications for your sexual health?

4

THE CHANGING REALITY OF HIV/AIDS

WORDS TO UNDERSTAND

AIDS: *Acquired immunodeficiency syndrome, a condition in which a person's immune system is so weakened that they become vulnerable to a wide range of diseases and infections.*

HIV: *Human immunodeficiency virus, a virus that attacks a person's immune system, causing AIDS.*

PEP: *Post-exposure prophylactic, a medical treatment that a person can receive to prevent HIV infection after they have been exposed to the virus.*

PrEP: *Pre-exposure prophylactic, a medical treatment that a person can receive on an ongoing basis to prevent infection with HIV.*

UNDETECTABLE: *When a person's level of HIV is so low that tests are unable to find the virus; research shows that these people are unable to transmit HIV.*

When John was diagnosed with HIV, he didn't completely understand what that meant. He had friends who were HIV-positive, but they hadn't really discussed in depth how that had impacted their lives. He knew that medications had improved to the extent that few people in the United States still die from HIV/AIDS, but he didn't know how else it might impact his health. "I'd been out of the closet and part of the gay community for years," John says, "with several friends living with HIV, but I'm a little embarrassed to say that I was still pretty ignorant about it."

"I knew some of the history. I had seen movies and documentaries about the AIDS crisis in the '80s and '90s. Even though I knew the experience would be different for me, I felt the weight of that history when I was given my diagnosis."

HIV and AIDS are widely known—everyone knows what they are. But almost 40 years after the first cases of AIDS were diagnosed, there are still many misconceptions about the disease. Even among LGBTQ people, there is a large degree of ignorance about the thing that has affected the community so massively.

25 YEARS
SURVIVING
AIDS

HIV and AIDS are widely known, but
there are still many misconceptions
about the virus and the disease.

AIDS can manifest in many different ways in different people.

WHAT IS HIV/AIDS?

The first area of misunderstanding about HIV/AIDS is in the use of the words themselves. **HIV**, which stands for human immunodeficiency virus, refers to the virus itself. That's the pathogen that is transmitted from one person to another. **AIDS** stands for acquired immunodeficiency syndrome, which is the condition that results from the virus's destruction within the body.

You'll notice that both terms refer to the immune system. That's the part of the human body that the virus attacks. The virus tears the immune system down by attacking the T-cells that serve an essential role in fighting off disease and infection. When a person's immune system is sufficiently weakened, the person becomes prone to infections and diseases that our bodies normally fight off very easily. When a person begins to be sick from those other diseases, that's when they are said to have the condition known as AIDS.

It's a little bit confusing, but to put it more simply, HIV is what a person "catches" from another person. AIDS is when someone becomes sick after being infected with HIV.

AIDS can manifest in many different ways in different people. Since the function of HIV is just to weaken the immune system, the disease that makes the person sick is not HIV itself, but whatever disease or infection manages to sneak past the weakened immunity. Common symptoms and conditions that arise include pneumonia, rashes, open sores, cancer, tuberculosis, flu, digestive issues, weight loss, and neurological (brain) conditions. It's also common for a person to experience a bout of flu-like symptoms for a period of time shortly after infection, though that doesn't occur for everyone.

HIV can also be transmitted through hypodermic needles used in drug use.

HOW HIV IS TRANSMITTED

Another area of confusion in relation to the disease is about how it is transmitted. There are a number of ways a person can become infected with HIV. As the U.S. Department of Health and Human

The Science of
HIV/AIDS

Services Web site says, "HIV is spread only in certain body fluids from a person who has HIV. These fluids are blood, semen, pre-seminal fluids, rectal fluids, vaginal fluids, and breast milk." Saliva and tears are bodily fluids that do not lead to transmission.

Sex is the most discussed means of transmission and is the one that most commonly impacts the LGBTQ community. Contrary to some people's perception, it's possible to become infected from both homosexual and heterosexual sex. Research has shown that receptive partners in anal sex—what is often called the "bottom" in the gay community—and heterosexual women are more at risk of receiving transmission. But heterosexual men and insertive partners in anal sex—"tops"—are also at risk.

Another common way for HIV to spread is through blood. In the early days of AIDS, blood transfusions needed for medical purposes sometimes led to transmission, but it wasn't long before doctors realized this and began testing blood for the virus and put restrictions on who could donate blood.

The other way blood can transmit HIV is through the use of hypodermic needles used in drug use. In hospitals and doctors' offices, a new needle is used each time one is needed. For people who use them to take drugs through injection, needles are sometimes shared or reused. Some blood could be left in the needle, which then could infect the next person to use the it.

As the quote above says, a mother's breast milk is also a way for HIV to be transmitted, leading to the tragic situation of mothers accidentally infecting their infant children.

It's believed that the HIV virus crossed over into humans from chimpanzees.

THE AIDS CRISIS BEGINS

AIDS was first observed among gay men in large urban areas like New York City, Los Angeles, and San Francisco as they began to die from extremely rare infections and forms of cancer such as a type known

A Short History of AIDS

The history of HIV/AIDS is a very misunderstood subject. At the time of the first outbreak, it was believed that the virus was relatively new. It was in 1981 that the first cases were observed and documented, and that was the beginning of the worst parts of the outbreak and pandemic. At the time, it was believed that there had been a "Patient Zero" who had been the source and had spread the disease across the country. A flight attendant was identified as the man who had brought AIDS to many cities as he traveled for work.

But more recent research shows that "Patient Zero" was not the origin of the disease. Researcher David Quammen details the history of AIDS in his book *The Chimp and the River: How AIDS Emerged From An African Forest*. He and other researchers have been able to track the surprisingly slow initial spread of the disease over many decades. It's believed that the virus crossed over into humans from a disease in chimpanzees through a hunter who was infected after he killed a chimp and managed to get blood from it into an open wound. Experts think that this occurred in Cameroon, in West Africa, around 1908, more than 70 years before HIV was first identified.

At the time—and for decades afterward—needles used for medical purposes were expensive, made of glass and metal. It wasn't possible to use a new needle every time one was needed. Researchers believe that the initial spread of HIV in West Africa, specifically in the city of Kinshasa in Congo, was caused by this needle sharing, as well as by sexual contact. The AIDS that resulted wasn't noticed because the life expectancy was extremely low, and it was very common for people to die from many other diseases and infections.

From West Africa, HIV spread to Haiti, which had a large degree of cultural interaction with Congo and a similarly short life expectancy, around 1960. It was around 1970 that AIDS made the jump to the United States, either from an individual immigrant or through a blood donation originating in Haiti. The virus was here from then on. It just wasn't until 1981 that the disease had reached enough people that a pattern was noticeable.

as *Kaposi's sarcoma.* Because that was the first population AIDS was observed in, it was originally called *gay-related immunodeficiency* or *GRID.*

It wasn't long before doctors and researchers realized that others were getting infected as well. They learned that the disease could be transmitted through both heterosexual and homosexual sex. Hemophiliacs were especially at risk of infection because they are more likely to need blood transfusions and sometimes that blood was infected. Drug users were also becoming infected through the sharing of needles used to inject drugs. It was after these discoveries that doctors began using the terms *HIV* and *AIDS* instead of *GRID.*

AIDS was first observed among gay men in large urban areas like New York City.

HOW HIV/AIDS AFFECTED THE GAY COMMUNITY

The impact of the AIDS crisis on the gay rights movement cannot be overstated. The onset of the epidemic came just as the movement was really taking off. The Stonewall Riots in New York City, considered the informal start of the gay rights movement, had taken place in 1969, just about a decade earlier. Activists were having some success in helping people see their LGBTQ friends, family members, and neighbors as people worthy of respect and civil rights. The AIDS crisis

The impact of the AIDS crisis on the gay rights movement cannot be overstated.

brought with it a renewed and even stronger fear of LGBTQ people, particularly of gay men. Some people were left with the impression that a person could get AIDS through everyday interaction with gay people. They became afraid to shake hands with gay men—even using the same public toilet scared people. There was also a moralistic element to it; some people believed that AIDS was God's punishment of gay people (ignoring all of the heterosexuals, even children, who were also dying). AIDS was a major setback for the movement.

Even more tragically, many of the LGBTQ movement's strongest voices were lost in the epidemic. Many of the activists who had dedicated their lives to promoting gay rights died during the 1980s and 1990s, their cries for equality forever silenced.

At the same time, the AIDS crisis brought new awareness to the lives (and, sadly, deaths) of gay people. Though some judged the people who were dying, some others were moved by compassion to see the tragedy of what was happening and realize that those who were dying were human as well. Awareness was also brought to the sexuality of public figures who might not otherwise have discussed their private lives. Celebrities, such as the actor Rock Hudson and the singer Freddy Mercury, were only found to have been gay by the general public because they died of AIDS.

Celebrities, such as the singer Freddy Mercury, were only discovered by the general public to have been gay because they died of AIDS.

Another way the AIDS crisis changed the gay community was by uniting it behind a common cause. New activist groups arose to fight for awareness of what gay people were going through, most famously the group ACT UP, which staged demonstrations around the country. It also brought lesbians and gay men together in a way that had not happened before. Previously, there had been some separation between the two groups. But when gay men began dying and had no one to care for them, lesbian organizations stepped up to help care for them.

HIV/AIDS TODAY

As John discovered after his HIV-positive diagnosis, the world for "poz" people is very different from how it was in decades past. Medications have improved exponentially. Although no cure has been

Very few people in the United States die from HIV/AIDS today.

found to be widely successful, medications that keep the disease at bay are accessible to most Americans.

John was diagnosed during a routine STI test, something he underwent on a regular basis. As a result, he had not become sick (though he had experienced the flu-like symptoms that often occur after infection). His HIV was caught early. He immediately began medication and very quickly became **undetectable**. That means that the level of virus is so low in his body that it's impossible for tests to find it. He still goes in for check-ups every few months to get his blood tested, but ever since he first began medication, he has been undetectable with a strong immune system. In addition to a test for the viral levels in their bodies, HIV-positive people are tested for CD4 levels, meaning the number of T-cells in their bodies. "My CD4 levels have always been high, meaning that I have as strong of an immune system as someone who is HIV-negative," John says.

Research also shows that a person who is undetectable is unable to transmit the virus to others, which marks a profound shift in how HIV is treated and how transmission is prevented. To John, all of this drives home the importance of being tested on a regular basis. "Because it was caught early, my health was never impacted, and I was able to get to the point very quickly where I was unable to infect anyone else."

Unfortunately, not everyone gets tested on a regular basis, and some people wait until they are sick to discover their HIV status. Very few people in the U.S. die from HIV/AIDS today, but some people still get very sick before they seek treatment, which can have long-lasting effects on their health. According to the CDC, about 15 percent of HIV-positive people in the United States do not know they are positive. *Know your status!*

PEP, PrEP, AND PREVENTION

New options for the prevention of transmission of HIV are available that did not exist even just a few years ago. One of the most game-changing is called *pre-exposure prophylaxis*, or **PrEP**. Research has shown that taking certain HIV medications before being exposed to the virus makes transmission nearly impossible. The most commonly used drug for this purpose is sold under the brand name Truvada, and more and more health providers are getting on board with the preventive benefits of the treatment. If you think you are at risk of getting HIV, you should ask your doctor about the possibility of taking PrEP.

Another option available to people is called *post-exposure prophylaxis*, or **PEP**. If a person believes that they have been exposed to HIV, they should talk to a doctor about the possibility of taking PEP. It is a course of medication taken beginning within 72 hours of the exposure (the earlier, the better), which is sometimes able to prevent the infection from taking hold. People sometimes use this option in case of a broken condom or being the victim of sexual assault.

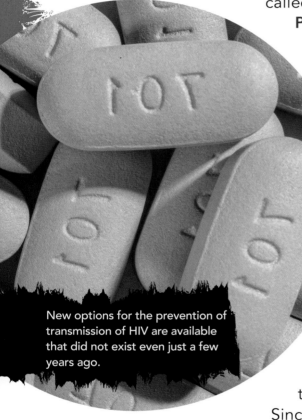

New options for the prevention of transmission of HIV are available that did not exist even just a few years ago.

In addition to PEP and PrEP, the best prevention is still the good-old-fashioned condom. Since HIV, like other STIs, is transmitted through the exchange of bodily fluids, minimizing the amount of interaction with someone else's fluids, like semen, reduces the chances of getting the virus. It should also be pointed out that PEP and PrEP do not prevent any other type of STI. Many health care professionals are beginning to advise the

HIV is a completely different issue from what it was in the past.

use of PrEP and condoms together to make HIV infection essentially impossible.

HIV is a completely different issue from what it was in the past. But despite this new world, it's still important for queer people (particularly gay men and trans women) to understand the disease, how it works, how to prevent it, and its place in the history of the LGBTQ movement.

HIV/AIDS is on the way out but is not gone yet.

DECIDING TO TAKE PrEP

The decision to take PrEP, the medication regimen to prevent contracting HIV, is a deeply personal one. It means thinking clearly and honestly about one's risk for infection.

The writer Zachary Zane discussed his own decision to take PrEP in an article he wrote for Pride.com. Zachary identifies as bisexual, and as an MSM, he knows he has some risk. He points out that his decision was not driven by any personal experience with HIV or AIDS, since "This generation—my generation—did not grow up in the time of the AIDS epidemic. We were too young to remember what it was like during the '80s and '90s, and my knowledge of the epidemic stems from readings, movies like *The Normal Heart*, and stories from my uncle, who said about half of his friends died from AIDS during this time."

Despite that disconnection from the former horrors of the disease, Zachary sees PrEP in the context of the overall history of HIV/AIDS. "We are lucky to be living in a generation where HIV is no longer a death sentence. HIV is now a manageable chronic illness. . . . That said, HIV is preventable, and something we as members of the LGBT+ community, need to work towards eradicating."

HIV/AIDS is on the way out but is not gone yet. It must be taken seriously, and Zachary, for one, considers PrEP to be one way to help to put the final nails in its coffin.

TEXT-DEPENDENT QUESTIONS

1. What is the difference between HIV and AIDS?

2. How does the HIV virus affect the body?

3. How did HIV/AIDS affect the LGBTQ community?

4. What are some ways to lower a person's chances of being infected?

RESEARCH PROJECT

Use the CDC's HIV Risk Estimator tool—https://wwwn.cdc.gov/hivrisk/estimator.html—to explore the risk associated with different activities. Which activities create the greatest risk for infection? Which activities create the least?

5

Getting the Health Care You Need

WORDS TO UNDERSTAND

HIPAA: *Health Insurance Privacy and Access Act—the federal law that governs the privacy of medical records.*

TITLE X HEALTH SERVICES: *Clinics funded by the government for the specific purpose of family planning services, including sexual and reproductive health.*

An hour and a half of instruction in LGBTQ health issues in four years of medical school is what the New York Medical College required when Sarah Spiegel began studying there. Recognizing that it was not nearly enough for a segment of society that faces a number of unique health issues, Sarah went to the school's faculty and administration and

Young doctors often report being underprepared for treating LGBTQ patients.

petitioned them for more inclusion. Fortunately, the administration, faculty, and other students responded well, and the school has been working to improve its curriculum. "We're getting there, but it's slow," Sarah told NPR.

Although the exact amount of specific instruction varies among medical schools, the problem is a common one. Graduates often report being underprepared for treating LGBTQ patients. The students themselves have begun to push for change and are often successful, but the change is still in progress. That also means that there are a lot of practicing doctors out there who graduated during an earlier era and were not given the information they need to care for LGBTQ people, through no fault of their own. It doesn't mean that LGBTQ people are unable to find proper health care. It just means that they sometimes have to look a little harder.

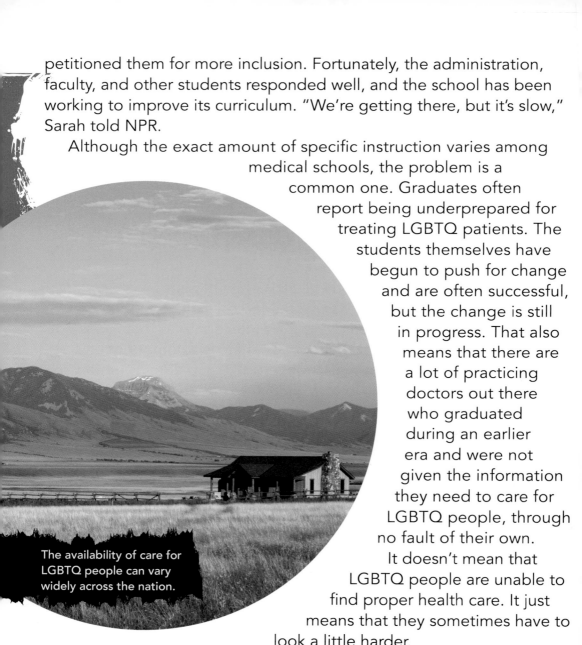

The availability of care for LGBTQ people can vary widely across the nation.

AVAILABILITY OF CARE FOR LGBTQ PEOPLE

For all the reasons discussed earlier, LGBTQ health issues are in many ways unique. LGBTQ people face some mental, physical, and sexual health issues that are less common for others. Risk factors for a number of conditions and diseases are different. That can make it more difficult to find health care services that are responsive to those specific needs. And it makes it useful to find health care professionals who are familiar with the particular needs of LGBTQ people.

Unfortunately, the availability of care for LGBTQ people can vary widely across the nation. It's a sad fact that someone living in rural Montana will have a much harder time accessing care specific to LGBTQ issues than will someone in New York City.

There are good online resources to help find health care providers who specialize in LGBTQ health issues.

FINDING A PROVIDER

Ideally, a young person would be able to ask at their school or local LGBTQ organization for help in finding LGBTQ-friendly health care services, but often that option is not available for young people.

Fortunately, some good resources exist online to help you find health care providers who specialize in (or at least are familiar with) LGBTQ health issues. One is www.glma.org, the Web site of the organization GLMA: Health Professionals Advancing LGBTQ Equality, which has a searchable database of LGBTQ-friendly providers. Go the homepage, and click on the "Find a Provider" button. The directory isn't comprehensive, but it could be a good place to start.

Another good way to start in finding a health care provider who is sensitive to LGBTQ issues is by checking out the CDC's "Get Tested" Web site, which includes a search engine for sexual health care providers. Its special emphasis is to help all people find STI testing services, not just LGBTQ people, but finding a sexual health care provider can be a good first step in identifying one who is familiar with LGBTQ issues. It's also great for finding a quick STI test, if that's all you're looking for. The search can also be useful in finding local LGBTQ organizations, as they are often listed as providers of HIV testing. The Web site is at www.gettested.cdc.gov.

Another useful Web site is https://opa-fpclinicdb.hhs.gov/, which is the U.S. Department of Health and Human Services' search tool for **Title X health services**. These are "family planning clinics." Planned Parenthood clinics are the most well-known examples, but there are many others. While they are especially well versed in women's and reproductive health issues, they are also just generally more likely to know about sexual health and to be sensitive to LGBTQ issues.

Planned Parenthood clinics are more likely to be sensitive to LGBTQ issues.

And then, of course, there is the low-tech strategy of just calling up a local provider and asking whether they have experience working with LGBTQ people or whether they feel comfortable doing so.

Once you find a place that works with LGBTQ people, they can help you find related services, like mental health care and counseling. For mental health especially, it's important to keep in mind that you should not settle for whomever you end up meeting with first. If the counselor or psychiatrist doesn't seem to be comfortable or familiar with LGBTQ issues—or even if you just don't gel—it's more than okay to try again with someone else. You can think of your first counseling session as a first date. It's okay if you aren't a perfect match. You're under no obligation to go on a second date.

HELP THEM HELP YOU

If you live in an area where none of these resources exists, it may be necessary to make do with what you have available to you. It can be intimidating to walk into a doctor's office if you think they aren't as educated as they could be about working with your health care needs.

As an LGBTQ person, it is sometimes necessary to help the doctor know how to help you. Since the doctor may not have been sufficiently trained in LGBTQ issues, they may not have all the information they need to treat you. That goes for physical health, sexual health, and mental health. It's an especially large problem for transgender patients who often have a hard time finding someone trained to help them. Of course, that's not always the case—plenty of doctors have become fully versed on the issues even if they weren't specifically taught about it in medical school—but you should be prepared just in case.

If a doctor doesn't seem to know enough about the subject of LGBTQ health care, you may have to give them some background information that you have. That could include the CDC's recommended tests listed in Chapter 3. You also may have to share how being LGBTQ has affected your mental health, any violence you have experienced as a result, self-image issues, or any other way your health has been affected that a non-LGBTQ person may not be aware of.

It's also common for doctors to overlook a young person's sexual history when performing a check-up. If you want to discuss sexual health issues with your doctor, you may have to be the one to bring it up. It's not an easy thing to do. It's often difficult to discuss sex with someone who is a stranger, let alone be the one to start the conversation. But it's important to take the initiative when your health is involved. Remember that you can also ask them a question they'll have to do some research on. It's okay to expect your doctor to learn a little in order to treat you.

One resource you may want to share with your doctor is www.lgbthealtheducation.org, a Web site made by health care professionals for health care professionals who need more information about the specific issues affecting LGBTQ people.

Don't let nervousness prevent you from seeking care. According to a study conducted by National Public Radio (NPR), "18 percent of all LGBTQ Americans refrain from seeing a physician for fear of discrimination." You don't want to be part of that number. Take control of your health.

If you want to discuss sexual health issues with your doctor, you may have to be the one to bring it up.

Coming out to your doctor helps you take control of your health care.

ALEX'S STORY OF COMING OUT TO HIS DOCTOR

Alex Galvan, a 20-year-old gay man living in a rural area of California, told NPR about how nervous he was to talk to his doctor about his sexual orientation and sex history. "He's going to flip out," Alex thought. "And then the moment before was, 'Oh gosh, here it goes.'" It felt like coming out all over again.

Alex was going to the doctor to ask for a prescription for PrEP, the HIV-preventive medication discussed in Chapter 4. The doctor didn't know what PrEP was but was willing to educate himself about it. In the end, Alex was glad he had done it because "coming out to his doctor is helping him take control of his life and health care."

For minors, accessing sexual health care can be a bit more complicated.

ACCESSING SEXUAL HEALTH CARE WHEN YOU'RE UNDER 18

For minors, the accessing of sexual health care can be a bit more complicated. For most medical care, it's assumed that parents will be kept in the loop of any tests or treatments that their child might receive. Ideally, young persons would be able to be as open and frank with their parents about their sexual health as they would be with any other aspect of their health. Ideally, parents would be supportive of their children receiving whatever care they might need. Unfortunately, that's not always the reality for young people.

But governments realize that in the case of sexual health, there are situations in which a minor should have a greater degree of control over their own health care decisions. According to the Guttmacher Institute, an organization that tracks sexual and reproductive health laws, "All states and D.C. allow young people to consent to STI services," meaning that no parental approval is necessary.

In other ways, state laws can vary considerably. Some states allow minors of any age to receive testing without parental approval. Others require persons to be over a certain age, usually 12 or 14, before they can decide for themselves to receive an STI test. Eighteen states allow, but do not require, a physician to inform a young person's parents that he or she is seeking or receiving STI services when the doctor deems it in the patient's best interests. If parents finding out about sexual health care is a concern, a person should do some research on their state laws. One good resource is the Guttmacher Institute's Web site, which has a complete breakdown of laws by state at www.guttmacher.org/state-policy/explore/overview-minors-consent-law.

Some states allow minors of any age to receive testing without parental approval.

ACCESS TO HEALTH INSURANCE

The ability of LGBTQ people to access health insurance through their spouses and partners is improving. Even before gay marriage became legal, many employers and some states were making it possible for LGBTQ people to share their insurance benefits with their family in a way that once had been available only to people in heterosexual relationships.

For people under the age of 18, health insurance can make accessing health care more complicated. Many young people are covered by their parents' health insurance, which is great except when it isn't. **HIPAA** (the Health Insurance Privacy and Access Act) is the federal law that governs

For people under the age of 18, health insurance (or the lack of it) can make accessing health care more difficult.

patient privacy. Its main purpose is to keep your health information—including medications, past illnesses, and treatments received—from being shared with anyone without your permission. That privacy is made more complicated when a health insurance policy is shared. Insurance companies usually send out an Explanation of Benefits (EOB) to the policy holder, explaining what services were provided and what the insurance paid for. That can lead to policy holders finding out what tests and treatments were given to the other people on their policy, which could undermine a person's privacy. According to the Guttmacher Institute, "13 states have provisions that serve to protect the confidentiality of individuals insured as dependents." To find out which protections are provided in your state, you can check out www.guttmacher. org/state-policy/explore/ protecting-confidentiality- individuals-insured- dependents.

If insurance is not an option for whatever reason, you might qualify for free or low-cost services at various health providers. The best way to know is just to call and ask.

Overall, accessing care for young LGBTQ people who are trying to look after their physical, mental, and sexual health can be a complicated process, but making sure you're healthy, and doing everything you can to stay that way, is worth it.

Making sure you're healthy, and doing everything you can to stay that way, should be your top priority.

TEXT-DEPENDENT QUESTIONS

1. What is HIPAA?

2. What subjects should you bring up when talking to your doctor?

3. What are some strategies for finding LGBTQ-friendly health services?

RESEARCH PROJECTS

1. Using the resources listed, find LGBTQ-friendly health services that are available in your area.

2. Imagine that you're going to a doctor who doesn't know anything about LGBTQ issues. What would you say, and what information would you provide, in order to help her or him meet your health care needs?

Agender (or neutrois, gender neutral, or genderless): Referring to someone who has little or no personal connection with gender.

Ally: Someone who supports equal civil rights, gender equality, and LGBTQ social movements; advocates on behalf of others; and challenges fear and discrimination in all its forms.

Asexual: An adjective used to describe people who do not experience sexual attraction. A person can also be aromantic, meaning they do not experience romantic attraction.

Asexual, or ace: Referring to someone who experiences little or no sexual attraction, or who experiences attraction but doesn't feel the need to act it out sexually. Many people who are asexual still identify with a specific sexual orientation.

Bigender: Referring to someone who identifies with both male and female genders, or even a third gender.

Binary: The belief that such things as gender identity have only two distinct, opposite, and disconnected forms. For example, the belief that only male and female genders exist. As a rejection of this belief, many people embrace a non-binary gender identity. (See **Gender nonconforming.**)

Biphobia: Fear of bisexuals, often based on stereotypes, including inaccurate associations with infidelity, promiscuity, and transmission of sexually transmitted infections.

Bisexual, or bi: Someone who is attracted to those of their same gender as well as to those of a different gender (for example, a woman who is attracted to both women and men). Some people use the word bisexual as an umbrella term to describe individuals that are attracted to more than one gender. In this way, the term is closely related to pansexual, or omnisexual, meaning someone who is attracted to people of any gender identity.

Butch, or masc: Someone whose gender expression is masculine. *Butch* is sometimes used as a derogatory term for lesbians, but it can also be claimed as an affirmative identity label.

Cisgender, or cis: A person whose gender identity matches the gender they were assigned at birth.

Coming out: The process through which a person accepts their sexual orientation and/or gender identity as part of their overall identity. For many, this involves sharing that identity with others, which makes it more of a lifetime process rather than just a one-time experience.

Cross-dresser: While anyone may wear clothes associated with a different sex, the term is typically used to refer to men who occasionally wear clothes, makeup, and accessories that are culturally associated with women. Those men typically identify as heterosexual. This activity is a form of gender expression and not done for entertainment purposes. Cross-dressers do not wish to permanently change their sex or live full-time as women.

Drag: The act of presenting as a different gender, usually for the purpose of entertainment (i.e., drag kings and queens). Many people who do drag do not wish to present as a different gender all of the time.

Gay: Someone who is attracted to those of their same gender. This is often used as an umbrella term but is used more specifically to describe men who are attracted to men.

Gender affirmation surgery: Medical procedures that some individuals elect to undergo to change their physical appearance to resemble more closely the way they view their gender identity.

Gender expression: The external manifestations of gender, expressed through such things as names, pronouns, clothing, haircuts, behavior, voice, and body characteristics.

Gender identity: One's internal, deeply held sense of gender. Some people identify completely with the gender they were assigned at birth (usually male or female), while others may identify with only a part of that gender or not at all. Some people identify with another gender entirely. Unlike gender expression, gender identity is not visible to others.

Gender nonconforming: Referring to someone whose gender identity and/or gender expression does not conform to the cultural or social expectations of gender, particularly in relation to male or female. This can be an umbrella term for many identities, including, but not limited to:

> **Genderfluid:** Someone whose gender identity and/or expression varies over time.

> **Genderqueer (or third gender):** Someone whose gender identity and/or expression falls between or outside of male and female.

Heterosexual: An adjective used to describe people whose enduring physical, romantic, and/ or emotional attraction is to people of the opposite sex. Also **straight**.

Homophobia: Fear of people who are attracted to the same sex. *Intolerance, bias,* or *prejudice* are usually more accurate descriptions of antipathy toward LGBTQ people.

Intergender: Referring to someone whose identity is between genders and/or a combination of gender identities and expressions.

Intersectionality: The idea that multiple identities intersect to create a whole that is different from its distinct parts. To understand someone, it is important to acknowledge that each of their identities is important and inextricably linked with all of the others. These can include identities related to gender, race, socioeconomic status, ethnicity, nationality, sexual orientation, religion, age, mental and/or physical ability, and more.

Intersex: Referring to someone who, due to a variety of factors, has reproductive or sexual anatomy that does not seem to fit the typical definitions for the female or male sex. Some people who are intersex may identify with the gender assigned to them at birth, while many others do not.

Lesbian: A woman who is attracted to other women. Some lesbians prefer to identify as gay women.

LGBTQ: Acronym for lesbian, gay, bisexual, transgender, and queer or questioning.

Non-binary and/or genderqueer: Terms used by some people who experience their gender identity and/or gender expression as falling outside the categories of man and woman. They may define their gender as falling somewhere in between man and woman, or they may define it as wholly different from these terms.

Out: Referring to a person who self-identifies as LGBTQ in their personal, public, and/or professional lives.

Pangender: Referring to a person whose identity comprises all or many gender identities and expressions.

Pride: The celebration of LGBTQ identities and the global LGBTQ community's resistance against discrimination and violence. Pride events are celebrated in many countries around the world, usually during the month of June to commemorate the Stonewall Riots that began in New York City in June 1969, a pivotal moment in the modern LGBTQ movement.

Queer: An adjective used by some people, particularly younger people, whose sexual orientation is not exclusively heterosexual (e.g., queer person, queer woman). Typically, for those who identify as queer, the terms *lesbian, gay,* and *bisexual* are perceived to be too limiting and/or fraught with cultural connotations that they feel don't apply to them. Some people may use *queer,* or more commonly *genderqueer*, to describe their gender identity and/or gender expression (see **non-binary** and/or **genderqueer**). Once considered a pejorative term, *queer* has been reclaimed by some LGBT people to describe themselves; however, it is not a universally accepted term, even within the LGBT community. When *Q* is seen at the end of LGBT, it may mean *queer* or *questioning*.

Questioning: A time in many people's lives when they question or experiment with their gender expression, gender identity, and/or sexual orientation. This experience is unique to everyone; for some, it can last a lifetime or be repeated many times over the course of a lifetime.

Sex: At birth, infants are commonly assigned a sex. This is usually based on the appearance of their external anatomy and is often confused with gender. However, a person's sex is actually a combination of bodily characteristics including chromosomes, hormones, internal and external reproductive organs, and secondary sex characteristics. As a result, there are many more sexes than just the binary male and female, just as there are many more genders than just male and female.

Sex reassignment surgery: See **Gender affirmation surgery**.

Sexual orientation: A person's enduring physical, romantic, and/or emotional attraction to another person. Gender identity and sexual orientation are not the same. Transgender people may be straight, lesbian, gay, bisexual, or queer. For example, a person who transitions from male to female and is attracted solely to men would typically identify as a straight woman.

Straight, or heterosexual: A word to describe women who are attracted to men and men who are attracted to women. This is not exclusive to those who are cisgender. For example, transgender men may identify as straight because they are attracted to women.

They/Them/Their: One of many sets of gender-neutral singular pronouns in English that can be used as an alternative to he/him/his or she/her/hers. Usage of this particular set is becoming increasingly prevalent, particularly within the LGBTQ community.

Transgender: An umbrella term for people whose gender identity and/or gender expression differs from what is typically associated with the sex they were assigned at birth. People under the transgender umbrella may describe themselves using one or more of a wide variety of terms—including transgender. A transgender identity is not dependent upon physical appearance or medical procedures.

Transgender man: People who were assigned female at birth but identify and live as a man may use this term to describe themselves. They may shorten it to *trans man*. Some may also use *FTM*, an abbreviation for *female-to-male*. Some may prefer to simply be called *men*, without any modifier. It is best to ask which term a person prefers.

Transgender woman: People who were assigned male at birth but identify and live as a woman may use this term to describe themselves. They may shorten it to *trans woman*. Some may also use *MTF*, an abbreviation for *male-to-female*. Some may prefer to simply be called *female*, without any modifier.

Transition: Altering one's birth sex is not a one-step procedure; it is a complex process that occurs over a long period of time. Transition can include some or all of the following personal, medical, and legal steps: telling one's family, friends, and co-workers; using a different name and new pronouns; dressing differently; changing one's name and/or sex on legal documents; hormone therapy; and possibly (though not always) one or more types of surgery. The exact steps involved in transition vary from person to person.

Transsexual: Someone who has undergone, or wishes to undergo, gender affirmation surgery. This is an older term that originated in the medical and psychological communities. Although many transgender people do not identify as transsexual, some still prefer the term.

FURTHER READING & INTERNET RESOURCES

BOOKS

Dawson, Juno. *This Book Is Gay*. Sourcebook Fire, 2015.

A wide-ranging handbook of what it's like to be LGBTQ. Includes information about sexual health but goes far beyond that as well, discussing everything from politics to puberty.

Engel, Jonathan. *The Epidemic*. HarperCollins, 2009.

A history of the AIDS crisis, from its origins to its role in the gay rights movement.

Langford, Jo. *The Pride Guide: A Guide to Sexual and Social Health for LGBTQ Youth*. Rowman and Littlefield, 2018.

A comprehensive guide to LGBTQ sexual health, including information about safer sex, dating, and relationships.

Savage, Dan, and Miller, Terry. *It Gets Better: Coming Out, Overcoming Bullying, and Creating a Life Worth Living*. Penguin Books, 2011.

From the couple who started the It Gets Better movement, this book includes essays from celebrities and regular people, too, describing how their lives have gotten better as they have left toxic environments behind.

WEB SITES

CDC Get Tested. https://gettested.cdc.gov/
The U.S. Centers for Disease Control and Prevention's page to assist people in getting tested for STIs. The site provides guidelines for which tests patients should request, as well as a tool for searching for providers.

CDC Lesbian, Gay, Bisexual, and Transgender Health. www.cdc.gov/lgbthealth/
The U.S. Centers for Disease Control and Prevention's page about LGBTQ health issues, including a wealth of information about their research and resources available to LGBTQ people. It includes a separate page of resources specifically for LGBTQ youth.

Human Rights Campaign. www.hrc.org
The HRC is a prominent LGBTQ rights organization that also conducts research on the community, including on health care issues. The Web site allows access to a wide variety of resources.

National LGBT Health Education Center. www.lgbthealtheducation.org
A Web site made specifically to provide information to health care providers about how to care for their LGBTQ patients. It could be a good resource to refer your doctor to if she or he doesn't have the information they need to treat you.

The Guttmacher Institute. www.guttmacher.org
The Guttmacher Institute is an organization that tracks laws regarding sexual and reproductive health. Its Web site provides information about its research, as well as information about laws and articles about current developments in sexual health policy.

The Trevor Project. www.thetrevorproject.org
The Trevor Project is an organization created to help young LGBTQ people who are struggling with mental health issues, particularly suicide prevention. In addition to a phone hotline and text line, the Web site provides people with the ability to talk to counselors over instant message. The Web site also provides other information about mental health.

INDEX

AUTHOR'S BIOGRAPHY

Jeremy Quist is a writer and California native. He conducted academic research on LGBTQ identity and community in Eastern Europe and wrote about his experiences at www.we2boys.com. He's lived throughout the western United States and now splits his time between Northern California and the road.

CREDITS

COVER

(clockwise from top left) iStock/asiseeit; iStock/martine Doucet; iStock/LightFieldStudios; iStock/FluxFactory;

INTERIOR